RTFM

Practical Advice for Smart Writers

Steven Greffenius

Puzzle Mountain Digital

Boston, Massachusetts

Contents

Introduction

No one would ever have tagged me as a future writer while I was still in school. I heartily disliked it, about as much as I disliked new math. Curriculum designers could make sex feel unnatural. They seem to be especially good at transforming something that should be fun into a chore. Some writing activities are in fact a chore, like washing dishes. You can't let stuff pile up in the sink. For the most part, writing is a great creative act. If you come out of school thinking otherwise, it's not your fault.

I gradually came to see the possibilities in writing when I arrived at my senior year in high school. Over the next decade and a half, I had the outstanding good fortune to work with writing teachers who understood the craft, and to know one person in particular who appreciates great writing. The hard work that goes into great writing began to seem less mysterious. I began to see how to build high quality written products, and came to appreciate their intrinsic value.

So let me tell you what this book is about. It is not about how to write fiction. I have written some poetry and dialogues, but I have not written short stories or novels. I don't know how to do that, and I don't know if I ever will. My training comes as an academic, and as a technical writer. Teachers call the documents non-fiction writers produce expository writing. They expose, or explain things. They uncover what lies underneath. Scientific writing does that, as does philosophical writing. Fiction does that too, of course, but storytelling does call for a different branch of writing skills.

As you look out and about, you'll see a lot of books about how to write fiction, fewer about how to write quality non-fiction. We all know how to write text messages, how to dash off a quick email message. We like to stay in touch, and fast food for the brain has something to recommend it. An old-school mind like mine will say that longer documents still have a place. We still need expository writing that extends beyond 140 characters, that amounts to more than captions for your daily life. These more extended written products require skill to construct. Like other skills, you have to learn them and practice them. You also have to adapt and extend the skills you have to new media, new purposes, and new expectations.

To take a simple example, the old-style paragraph we learned to write in school reached buggy-whip status as digital communications came to dominate. An old-style paragraph is about 150 words, has a topic sentence, and is structured as a mini-essay. Many schools still teach their students how to write paragraphs like that. Yet you go out to read real paragraphs, and you see that most of them are about half that long. They do not contain a key sentence that expresses the paragraph's central point. Often they do not even make an independent point, as you would expect from a mini-essay. Shorter paragraphs function as modest chunks in a larger structure – in length and in substance, they are something intermediate between a pair of sentences and an old-style, 150 word paragraph. This structural change represents a major transformation in the way we write, brought about because reading large chunks of text on a computer or mobile device is just not a desirable or pleasant thing to do. Therefore we use smaller chunks of text that communicate what we want to say.

For quite a while I thought, "I can't write for the web – I just can't learn to write paragraphs that short": the usual pessimistic, defeatist self-talk you engage in when you don't want to do something, and you need to justify your inactivity. Gradually I did learn, and discovered that these paragraphs are not so different from the ones I was writing for technical documents. Three or four sentences give you the rhythm you need for these shorter chunks.

That was just one evolution. The larger change in the writing landscape, of course, comes when you prepare documents for someone other than a teacher. That's a lot of years to practice, writing for an audience of one! You hand a paper in, and you get it back with a grade. At least you have direct contact with your audience – something you do not typically have with business or technical writing. Still, a larger, more remote audience has rewards, too. You know that what you write might actually help someone.

This essay about writing grows out of two parts of my life as a writer. During the first part, I was a young teacher, not long out of graduate school, paid to help undergraduate students in my classes improve their writing skills. Many classes were about politics, others were specially tailored to focus on writing. Either way, if I was in a position to grade student papers, I wanted to do what I could to make their work easier, as well as mine. My own mental health was at stake! I sometimes commented that spending a couple of hours grading essays could turn your brain to mush. It seemed like a needless consequence. I knew my students could write better quality stuff. So I gave a short chalk talk, in the manner of a coach, to communicate the steps students should take as they prepared their papers. From the quality of the papers I read, most students did not follow my advice. That did not deter me. I kept giving my talk. I noticed that if a student took more than one class with me, that student's writing often improved. I remember one student who had not had good training with short compositions in high school. His early work was not good. He tried hard, and his improvement over two or three semesters reflected his effort. That was enough. Teachers will tell you that. If you can make a positive difference for even one student, that is sufficient.

The second part of this essay grows out of a talk I gave to a professional group after working for quite a long time as a technical writer. I will tell you that a great deal of technical writing is not like normal writing. Then again, just as with people, what is normal? *Normal* is just a concept we use to make invidious comparisons. If you don't like invidious comparisons, throw out the concept. In any case, for technical documents, you need a set of skills you readily develop as an academic writer, but applied in a business environment. The two fields – academic and technical writing – do have a lot in common. Because both types of writing capture a number of the positive qualities required to succeed with non-fiction publications, and because the methods writers use in both fields are also similar, it is not so difficult to talk about the two together, and to extend these thoughts to other non-fiction writing projects. If you want to tell stories, you would not go to a technical writer or editor for help. If you want to organize a large quantity of complicated information, to make it accessible to people who are new to a field, a technical writer is the first place you would go for help. Just as we have software architects, we have information architects, one of those job titles that did not take off, but that captures the author's contribution well enough. You want the structure of your language to parallel its purpose.

Take a little time to think about what you read here, especially if you want to improve your craft. I did not tell my students often enough: if you want to succeed in the working world, learn to write well. People who don't learn that skill do not get promotions or pay increases. Good writing leads to good speaking: both lead to effective persuasion, and simply the ability to get things done. This whole basket of skills and qualities – the ability to communicate and get things done – is in demand everywhere. That's why you see it on every job description. The hiring manager really means it: the company wants someone who can communicate well! If their candidates routinely had those skills, they would not bother to list it. Inside a company, I am struck by the extreme range of quality in written communication, and the large contribution that good writing makes to a company's success. No wonder managers value the ability, and look for it. Everyone needs good writers, because good writers know how to think.

One more piece of advice, before we enter the forest. Look for chances to practice. If this were a different book – a workbook rather than a medium-length essay – I could include writing exercises to let you try out the different methods I discuss. It's not a workbook, though, and I don't want to give the essay too much of a classroom air. I feel comfortable with more personal memories, which I hope help you to recall your experiences with writing, in school and elsewhere. Spend time with pieces of language longer than a text message or a tweet. The longer the piece, the more opportunity you'll have to think and learn. Give yourself an opportunity to communicate complicated thoughts. Skills required to do so follow from practice, as will your sense of accomplishment and satisfaction.

Zen of Writer's Block

Writer's block is a famous concept easily misunderstood. You can't say the phenomenon is fictitious: projects are often hard to start, you can tell yourself you have nothing to say, a blank sheet of paper – or its digital equivalent – may make you think your mind has gone blank as well. These are not problems unique to writers, or to habitual procrastinators, or to people who have blank minds. Of course, if you turn inward to find your mind blank all the time, you may have achieved Zen mastership without all the arduous training that usually requires.

For the rest of us, go online to find advice about how to overcome writer's block. These tips have a certain amount of value, but at bottom, problems getting started come from having some ill-defined purpose that does not compel you to write something *now*. Some situations hand you a purpose. Suppose you plan to give a talk before a large group of strange people: will you write some notes, or stand at the lectern with nothing to say? A teacher assigns a paper for your class: will you start the paper, or receive an F for the assignment? Your boss needs you to write a report to prepare a presentation for senior management: do you write the report, or tell your boss you really don't think you want to do that right now? These examples illustrate how external circumstances can create a compelling sense of purpose.

Writer's block occurs when a well-defined, compelling sense of purpose does not exist. If external circumstances do not create it, you must create it on your own. Pretend someone wants to pay you for your output, that you will disappoint your parents, or that some bad thing must happen if you do not manage to produce something. Make-believe urgency may come to feel like the real thing, especially if you promise results to your friends, your colleagues, your family, or your alter ego.

Suppose you have a sense of purpose, howsoever it originates. Now answer two questions while you think about what to write: 1) Who will read it? 2) Why do you want them read it? If you answer the first question in the first person, you need not consider the second question. People write many things they don't read later. If you intend your thoughts for someone else, consider both questions. You needn't answer them before you write, but you should know the answers when you finish. Whether you want to post a small sign that contains less than ten words, write an essay of 7,000 words, or write a 350 page novel, have a purpose. Translate your purpose into a sense of your audience: who cares about what you write, and why?

When you do that, writer's block goes away. It's true a lot of things other than writer's block can make you procrastinate. Deferral mechanisms come in many forms. Procrastination is not *writer's* block per se. If you want to write – now – and the blank page still stares you down, it generally means you have not brought *who* and *why* into sufficient focus. If asking the questions in your head does not yield satisfactory results, write each question down: *1) Who will read this? 2) Why will they read it?* The second question points to a third, closely related prompt: what do I want to accomplish here? If that form of the question feels more appropriate, concentrate your effort there. Write your answers. Then you'll be ready to begin. Your sheet of paper won't be blank anymore, either.

In the first part of this section, I avoid specific advice about how to deal with writer's block. The second part suggests some specific practices. Best of all is to develop practices where you generally don't have to deal with writer's block at all. I have a terrible time with procrastination on big projects – books I write for myself, not for a client – but for me procrastination masks other problems. Classic writer's block refers to that dammed up feeling you have when you cannot express your thoughts, thoughts so clear they feel musical while still inside your head.

Perhaps I'm mistaken about the distinction between procrastination and writer's block, but mostly I have way too much to say. That means I have to manage my writing time to concentrate on what's most important. Of course I have the experience – quite often – of thinking eloquent thoughts that just don't flow from the keyboard. That's painful. It's part of writing. On the other side, you often see things flow from the keyboard that you did not expect. That's joyful. You do have to be confident that, if you think about something long enough, you'll eventually be able to write about it, and write well.

The first three pieces of advice below deal with thought processes. If you don't think, you can't write. If you don't communicate – speak, read, write, and listen – you'll eventually stop thinking. You have to keep your mind fertile with regular, high quality communication.

- *Read.* Every book or article about how to write well includes this advice. You absolutely cannot become a good writer if you do not read. Structurally, reading and writing lie closer to each other than they do to speaking and listening. Reading a lot is the single most important activity you can undertake to avoid writer's block.

- *Think.* Think about subjects that engage you as you apply yourself to other activities. Your brain is on automatic for many of the things you do during the day. Think about things that are important to you during these times. The more you think about something, the more readily you can write about it.

- *Talk and listen.* Even though oral communication differs from written communication, it's still essential for keeping your mind active, learning, and growing. Conversation and other forms of oral communication contribute a great deal to your ability to write fluently. Writing may be a solitary activity, but good writing grows from all kinds of interaction with other people.

The second trio of items addresses the sometimes difficult task of expressing thoughts inside your mind, in language entirely accessible to other people.

- *Regular habits.* As with the first point about reading above, you'll see this advice a lot. Have a routine that makes you productive. Regular habits often mean writing at the same time and same place every day, but modern, mobile schedules may interfere with that. The best you can do is be conscious of routines, then develop habits that contribute to the kind of writing you want to do.

- *Physical activity.* This item is extremely important to me. I am a restless person. More generally, the brain needs physical activity in order to work properly. Whatever mental activities you have before you, your brain will thank you for the extra oxygen and nutrients you supply by taking a walk, or doing anything else that helps circulate your blood vigorously. We can't avoid sitting, but we need not sit more than necessary.

- *Chicken scratches.* This activity represents the last preparatory stage, a transition state between fleeting thoughts and written language. Below I've devoted a couple of paragraphs to this activity.

The formal term for chicken scratches is *pre-writing*, or simply *notes*. You know from years in school that notes can vary a great deal. They may contain diagrams, arrows, lists, tables, references, phrases, points of emphasis, sentence fragments, abbreviations, symbols, marginal comments, asides, unconventional punctuation, all manner of disorder, and few signs of order. Why, you think, is my brain so disorganized? It's not disorganized. It's simply wired for associative memory and communication. Pre-writing creates a transition between this type of neural network, and the far different rules of structure we use for written communication.

I use a form of speed writing for my notes, where many of the marks on my notepad resemble chicken scratches. A lot of people don't write notes on paper anymore, and have developed alternate ways to set down initial thoughts. Whatever your method or medium, the central verbal function of notes is constant: set jumbled thoughts on a path to organization. No one else will see these notes. No one else could ever understand them, so you have taken external judgment out of the process. All you have to do is place the tip of your pen on your pad, even if your mind feels blank or dammed up, and see what happens.

Writing Process Chalk Talk

Back when I taught writing to young college students, I gave what I called a chalk talk to help them prepare the semester's first paper. I intended it as a quick refresher about how to write a short paper, and an introduction to my own standards of evaluation. Class members would understand that if they did not take enough care with their writing, it would be obvious to me.

I did then, and still do, believe heartily in the efficacy of sound methods. If the process is sound, so is the product. If you follow the recipe, you'll have a good meal at the end. I called my method the writing function machine, a name intended to emphasize the method's mechanical nature. Here's the recipe. Follow it and you will have good results.

Function machine also recalls high school algebra. We all remember $y = f(x)$, a formulation that appears useful only for mathematicians until you draw it:

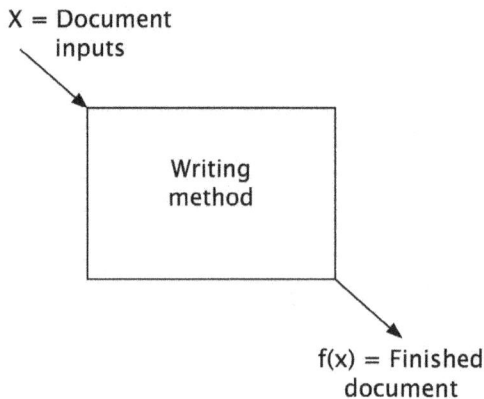

X = Document
inputs

Writing
method

f(x) = Finished
document

Preparing a paper isn't that mechanical, and writing methods certainly do not follow a straight line, but the idea still works. Start with your thoughts and your plans for a project, run these inputs through the right process, then deliver your output: a paper that expresses your thoughts with enough clarity that someone else understands them. You need not have doubts about your output's quality if you have confidence in the process.

Every writer creates in a different way. These various methods have elements in common, but key advice is to do what works best for you, based on your own habits, training, and requirements of the particular project in front of you. Meantime, the process sketched out in the chalk talk serves well as an all-purpose start. It's a readily adaptable framework.

Remember, too, we want a method to compose a short paper, often two to three pages, sometimes three to five pages. For papers this short, a simple five-step process comprehends the entire recipe. The process is not recursive, nor do processes run in parallel. You do not want to impose a complicated development process on a short work product due in just a few days, or on writers who are beginners. You can apply more complicated methods to longer pieces later on.

These five steps, then, make up the writing process:

1. Write notes.
2. Outline.
3. Rough draft.
4. Revise.
5. Proofread.

Let's consider each of these steps with sufficient care in the next two sections.

Pre-Write to Get Started

The first two steps comprise pre-writing: preparatory activities you undertake before you write an initial draft. These two steps vary the most from writing project to writing project, and from writer to writer. You have to think about what works best for you, in light of your goals for the project, and your goals for the audience.

Write notes. The notes you write may or may not look like chicken scratches. Either way, note writing fills a lot of needs, especially brainstorming to fuel creativity. Write whatever comes into your head, or think for a bit, then write what comes into your head. Go for a walk to clear your head, and let your thoughts form naturally as you stride along. Read *Zen of Writers Block* for more on how to get started.

My daughter writes a lot for school. She's fluent and thoughtful, but she doesn't write notes. Sometimes she despairs just at the point where words need to appear on the paper, where you can tell from what she says that she has formulated her thoughts well. I'll say, "Just write down anything. It doesn't matter what you say. Once you've done that, you'll have something to work with." – like clay for a potter, or wood for a carpenter. She rejects the advice vehemently, so I don't say it anymore. Eventually she writes. After so many papers, I still don 't understand how she gets started. I guess she just thinks until she's ready to write. The brief despair activates her fingers on the keyboard.

I tell this story mostly to say that writers and writing projects differ. When I begin to write a short post on politics for my blog, I just write, in well-formed sentences. That feels natural because I have thought about the subject for a long time. When I launch a writing project on a technical subject, where I have to learn how something works from scratch, I write more notes than I care to say. The first legal pad fills up; I reach for a second. The pads contain meeting notes, interview notes, questions, planning notes, more questions, partial answers to questions, references to source material, and so on.

Outline. I urged students to write an outline, even though I do not like to write them myself. We can all tell when an author has not given sufficient thought to organization. Presenting your thoughts in the proper order is a difficult problem to solve. You cannot readily solve that problem while you think about what you actually want to say, especially when the subject matter is unfamiliar. You need a map to indicate what comes first, what comes next, what comes after that. In a short composition, an outline directs your thoughts in an orderly manner toward your conclusion. Without this self-imposed direction, your readers will not even know why you have written down anything at all, because you have arrived nowhere, and have not communicated anything coherent. Your composition barely progresses past the notes stage. You may save yourself some work when you don't organize your thoughts, but the work you do goes to waste.

I need to add a couple of major qualifiers here. The method we learned to write an outline in school can put you off. They feel like too much trouble. You wind up thinking," I'll do anything to avoid this step." That applies to me. I have not written a formal outline in advance of my rough draft for some time. I do like lists and associated planning notes, I do like to create empty buckets in my draft, and I do generate my table of contents frequently, to show the current structure of my project. You can find workarounds if you don't want to create a well formed outline in advance.

The second qualifier speaks to the way your brain works. You cannot write an accurate outline before you start to write. The only accurate outline reflects the structure of the finished product. During document development, you have to go back and forth between the outline and the draft taking shape, to modify each in light of the other. As you write, you'll know when you need to revisit or consult your outline, to remind yourself what's next, and to modify your map to reflect the new directions you have taken and the new content you have developed. After you have written some pretty rudimentary planning notes, your outline changes and takes shape along with the draft. I think of it as a reflective process, with the outline above and the draft below. The outline functions as a key planning document, but the writing process, with all of its complications, affects the content of the planning document a great deal.

Now we have discussed the first two steps, which in formal terms is the pre-writing stage. Notes and outline both involve a lot of writing, of course, but it's not the standard activity required to prepare a rough draft. Pre-writing is actually quite enjoyable, if you understand why you are doing it. This two-step, preparatory phase supplies raw material – notes – and a plan – a cheat sheet if you like that we used to call an outline in school. With all of that in hand, writing rapidly and naturally to prepare a rough draft becomes a smooth, almost pleasant activity.

Write Rapidly, Rewrite, Copyedit

Rough draft. The main thing to remember about your first draft is, write it fast. Don't pause over punctuation, word selection, phrasing, sentence structure or rhythm, clear meaning, consistent terminology, paragraph divisions, or anything that can slow you down as you fill your page with words. Remember, the scariest thing in the world for a writer is the blank page. It stares at you with one message: you don't have anything to say. You know the message isn't true, but it becomes true if you stare for even a few moments. It interrupts your thoughts and makes you into the world's most renowned procrastinator. So don't ever let yourself face a blank page. Start with a page that has something on it already. If you encounter a clean page, put something on it as fast as you can. Then keep writing.

Rapid writing has another virtue. It can lead to freshest expression of the thoughts inside your mind. Yes, fresh expression does not always mean clear expression, but clarity can come later. For the first draft, you want original, dew-on-the-grass thoughts – opposite the dry, stale language you may craft when you become overly conscious of your audience, and your audience's expectations. Like clarity, audience response comes later. You may not be writing entirely for yourself anymore, but if you pause to think during your initial draft, prod yourself to keep writing. Pause too long, and you may find you have lost your tailwind. Suddenly you are dead in the water, or barely going anywhere. Everyone understands that momentum matters. That principle applies especially to things like first drafts.

You may think, "You're telling me to ignore too much," or, "That's just not how I work." Fair enough: I like to get it right, too. Nevertheless, you have ample time and space to get it right in step four. Just as writing notes and planning your project differ from drafting, drafting differs from revising. The reason for process is to separate activities that must be done in sequence, not together. If you try to do them at the same time, you run into trouble. If you try to formulate every sentence just so in your head, writing becomes an agony. It is supposed to flow, like water over rocks in a stream. If you dam up the stream, you have predictable results: a big pool of stagnant water rather than a waterfall. Go for the immediacy, motion, and impact of a waterfall when you create your initial draft.

Revise. I built a kayak with a friend not long ago. Roughing out the hull was quite remarkable. One day you have all these pre-cut pieces and plans lying flat in your workspace. The next you have something that looks like a boat, and you can set many of your drawings aside. Now the painstaking work begins: many hours of sanding, finishing, fiber glassing to add strength and make the boat waterproof. You have a lot of satisfaction seeing the hull take shape, but you are still a long way from having a boat you can put in the water.

Still, the finishing process – what writers call revising – is not so painful as it might sound. You have confidence now that you have something worth working on. The words are outside of you, ready for you to manipulate them. Sometimes I go to work on the notes from step one. In that case I massage them into shape, where clay is a closer metaphor than a wooden structure. Other times I work on a rough draft, so the metaphor of sanding wood and finishing it applies. Either way, revision is a stage where you can feel like a craftsman, take pride in your craft, and pay attention to the many elements you deliberately ignored during the rapid writing phases.

Here are a few tips for revision. Your schedule may not allow for all of these. Reading your words aloud may be one of those things you just don't want to do, if no one will ever present the work in front of an audience. Still, these techniques can help you make rapid progress with your draft:

- Come back to your draft after some time away from it. Then you can approach the work as if it belongs to someone else, and you can become your own best critic.
- Read your work aloud, with a pen handy to make notations. This technique is essential if you plan to present your work as a speech.
- Think of revision as rewriting, not just fixing things up:
  o Delete unnecessary text, no matter how short or long.
  o Add new paragraphs and sentences: any material required to spell out your meaning.
  o Move stuff around.
  o Write and rewrite until the text reads just the way you want it to.
- Stick with revision. Copyediting comes in step five.
- Put the draft, or each section of the draft, through as many iterations as necessary.

The last point bears on when to bring revision to a close. You'll know when you have reached a point where the project schedule and clarity of expression meet. That is when time is short, and the writing is of high enough quality to accomplish its purpose.

Proofread. After four such demanding steps, one wants an easier fifth step. Proofing is the word we used back in the days of print, when you would check the printer's proofs for errors before you sent them out for the print run. If you didn't catch the error at that point, it would be reproduced everywhere and forever. Not so much with digital publications, where you can catch an error and correct it anytime.

Nevertheless, you do not want errors in your finished product. Three good reasons exist:

- They take time and trouble to correct down the line, when you want to be working on other things.

- They distract readers. Readers start to think about errors rather than what you want to communicate.

- They destroy your readers' confidence in the accuracy of the entire publication.

Altogether, errors show carelessness and lack of attention to detail. Readers ask, if the publisher could not catch this error, what else in there isn't right? Readers can even lose interest in the technical information you want them to know.

I made reference above to copyediting. In the old days, checking proofs was no time to introduce corrections for anything but out-and-out errors. Printers expected finished copy when they set up their proofs. Now, copyediting and proofreading tend to be combined in the same step. Copyediting makes sure punctuation is just right, the document conforms to the company's style guide, no loose ends from previous reviews remain, and so on. Digital publication processes give editors more latitude to make changes and corrections right up until publication, and of course even after publication if the company and its staff want that.

Do not stint on this last stage, then. For long, complicated documents, a single checklist can help. Check pagination, table of contents, headers and footers, placement of tables and figures, and so on. You want to make sure *you* discover problems, not your readers. Of course, getting feedback from readers is a great channel of communication to keep open. Nevertheless both parties ought to use the channel to communicate about substantive technical questions, not pesky mistakes.

So that summarizes the five step process. Back when I first put together this chalk talk, most of the writing I had done was academic, one way or another. I had been a student for so many years, and so many classes. At the time, I was an instructor with responsibility to help my students become confident writers themselves. I had to evaluate and write comments for their papers. My role as instructor, coach, and grader gave me more pleasure, and sense of efficacy, if I could help students achieve a basic standard of quality in their papers. They could achieve that standard if they knew how to go about the writing process. Since then, I see the variability of form, scale, and purpose in writing projects. Every project has its own requirements, which in turn affect the document's development process. Add in variability in writer's preferences and habits, and you could say no one can talk about one writing process.

Strictly speaking, that is correct. Nevertheless, if you generalize the process enough, allow for variability and adaptation, and consider what a good written product requires, you can see why the process outlined here has value. If you keep these methods in mind, you have a good foundation. People joke about learning to cook, "I can't even boil water." Well of course you can heat water to make something warm. Similarly, people are born with a need to communicate, so writing comes naturally. Just as we know the difference between boiled potatoes and dinner served by a great chef, we come to appreciate the care required to prepare a complex publication. Chefs learn to cook when they follow recipes, then become accomplished enough to write their own. Young writers may feel the recipes their instructors give them are rather confining, but still know the freedom of a rather less structured writing process soon enough. Meantime, fundamental skills they learned early will help them improve their craftsmanship later on. You know that if you run through the process, you'll have a good product.

How Can I Manage My Content Effectively?

One title for this section might be, *Help your clients manage digital content (they won't do it on their own)*. If you are a consultant, in particular a consulting engineer, you have a lot of documents – digital content – to manage as part of the projects you undertake. So I wanted to give a little thought to this subject. The first thing to say is that the parenthetical part of the title conveys a little humor, but it's not demonstrably true. People manage digital content the best they can. Often they have to do it on their own, since no one will do it for them. Moreover, companies, teams, project managers, and technical types generally run the full range in the care they take with document management. You cannot say with facile assurance, people won't do it on their own.

Having said that, the full range of processes and outcomes for digital content is large, with many companies unhappy about their performance in this difficult area. The goal for such systems is simply stated: create and deliver correct information, to the person who needs it, at the required place and time. If your content creation processes fail, it does not matter how well your delivery channels function. If your delivery channels fail, it does not matter how well your content creation processes function. You have to couple the two parts together tightly.

Practical Questions

That's a general introduction. Now let's have a look at some of the practical questions you want to ask when you undertake a new project. Sometimes the tools and processes you use are in-house. In that case, they may not change from project to project. If you work as a consultant, you must adapt your work methods to accommodate your client's established processes. Here are three questions that arise for both kinds of projects:

- What tools will I use to create content?
- What tools will I use to manage content?
- What content management processes are in place?
- What file formats are in play?

I've stated these questions as simply as I can, but you can see that for large companies, the way content management works can become complicated pretty quickly. Even for a small project team, proper content management can become troublesome if people do not think about the problem.

Let's take the second question as an illustration. Then let's narrow that question down to the problem of version control. Later, I'd like to compare the way software developers handle source control with the way document developers handle version control. They are not the same thing, though they both involve similar techniques and goals. For now, we'll consider the question that comes up at the beginning of a project: What tools will I use to manage content?

If you are the only person who will ever handle the document, the answer to that question is easy. We all have a file structure on our local drives, file naming conventions, and more or less rational routines to make sure we don't lose data. Losing data is the great bugaboo of modern office life. We build our processes so it does not happen, because we have difficulty doing our jobs when it does happen.

As soon as you create a document for other people, you have to think about basic document management questions. Simple questions, such as where the date appears, must be addressed. Does the document need a version number? Whether or not a number is assigned, how is versioning of the document handled? If applicable, at what point in a document's development is a version number assigned? Lastly, how do answers to these questions about dates and version numbers affect file naming conventions?

You want to glance at a document in a data storage system, whether it's on your local drive or on a server, and determine immediately whether it's the document you want. If you murmur in objection, "When I start a project, I don't want to think about file names right off the bat," think about what happens when you don't. Requirements of modern data retrieval systems force you to have methods that work. Recall that business firms in the 1930s hired armies of clerks whose only job was to maintain the company's data retrieval system – that is, paper documents stored in filing cabinets. The need for proper control of digital content is far greater now, when you can't touch the documents, and content multiplies stupendously.

Content Management Systems

We've come a fair distance without talking about the tools we use for version control. They vary a lot, and none is perfect. Some content management systems, such as Microsoft's SharePoint or Drupal, are designed from the start as document control software. Others, such as CVS (Concurrent Versioning System), are designed to handle source code in particular, but companies may use them for document control as well. Subversion, Perforce, and Team Foundation Server work reasonably well for code and content. Lastly, some companies use home grown content management systems. Watch out for these! These tools are hard to update.

Document managers, of course, feel most comfortable in an environment tailored for all kinds of document and image formats. Workflows for document control are not exactly the same as those for source code. If you are a software developer, you may not react negatively to a source control tool that emphasizes computer code over document files. All in all, if you have a lot of documents to manage, you want a content management system designed for content, whether the content is stored in tool-specific project files, .doc files, .pdf files, .html files, .xml files, or all the image file formats you can think of. You especially want a content management system – or version control system – that adapts well to all the processes in place to create, publish, and revise your content.

Note that when we talk about content management systems, or version control systems, we often think about tools designed for these purposes. That's natural enough. More broadly, though, you probably want to think about content management as a set of procedures or processes, where the tools in place determine some but not all of what's required to manage documents effectively. For instance, SharePoint as a web application is designed to store and manage content. When you use SharePoint, you have to observe the specific procedures required within SharePoint to accomplish a task. Yet the most effective method is to decide what procedures *you* want to use, then decide what tools and practices you want to implement in light of that.

Once again, toolsets, version control systems, or large content management systems cannot determine all of what's required to meet the goals of document control. Tool vendors may claim that their product or service will solve all of your content management problems for you, but in fact you still have to give some independent thought to these problems. Practical solutions to create and deliver content, when and where it's needed, cannot come from an application. The toolset has to work for the company and its project teams, not the other way around. If you are not careful, you can become so absorbed in making the tools work that your team's creative energy dissipates.

What does that mean for consultants? First is to be conscious of how many tools for content management exist. Second is to remember that companies generally don't give as much thought to content management problems as they do to, say, sales or customer support. That is true even though effective document management is integral to superior customer support. Third is to know that you can adapt your work methods to accommodate your client's processes for document control. Your client will not change its document control processes to accommodate you.

Nevertheless, you may sometimes be struck by how broken and ineffective the processes in place can be.

In the end, document control places demands on companies they are not well equipped to meet. You want to manage change in your library as well as change in the methods you use to mange your library. The interplay between fluid content, and procedures that evolve as firms grow, never disappears or abates. Compare these challenges with financial accounting. Business accounting practices have had several centuries to evolve. Companies rely on well proven practices to track and fund global operations. Procedures for document management in the digital age have had only a few decades to evolve. Consider how recently we used card catalogs in libraries. Some regard content management as an extension of writing, but in several important respects, document control requires other skills. Large companies commonly overlook the need for these skills in their organizations.

Some companies have developed more effective practices than others. Almost all companies recognize that problems of document control are not as easy as they may have looked at first. You cannot merely assign a document number to a file, store the file in your database, then retrieve it later on if you need to have another look at it. If you leave it at that, you end with a largely static pile of outdated files, rather than a flexible management system. Companies know that if their document control systems do not take change into account – if they are not streamlined and adaptable – they just slow the company up and demoralize its people. Those outcomes make companies ill equipped to match their competitors' success.

Seven Principles for Effective Document Development

A lot of good advice exists about principles of good writing – imperatives for sentence structure, and so on – but practical advice about how to handle documents effectively is harder to find. Moreover, we can find scads of how-to help for authors who want to write and publish fiction, but less in that line for writers who work for businesses, and who write as a business. Here are seven useful principles to guide business document development:

1) Think about what you want to write as you plan it. That seems self-evident, but the mechanics of planning – simply preparing a document plan or an outline and getting it approved – replaces adequate thought about the document's contents. Frame your thinking about content with two questions. First, who will consult the document? Second, why will your audience consult it, which is another way to ask, what is your purpose?

2) Do adequate research. You do not need to know everything about a subject to write about it. You only need to know enough to meet the requirements inherent in your purpose. Moreover, if you know your audience well enough to know what information they need, and why they need it, you can identify what you need to know as a writer. Once you get started with research, you can formulate questions about what you want to learn.

3) Organize your material. Your table of contents contains a list of top-level headings, to summarize major pieces of your document. You may think it exists to help your readers, but readers will go first for the search field. For long documents, the table of contents exists especially to help you. During document development, the table of contents displays the document's overall structure for you, and for the whole development team. Use it as your outline. Look for ways to improve your document's organization as the amount of content grows.

4) *Solicit feedback early and often*. Writers often don't like to submit work for review prematurely. They think it reflects poorly on their own skills if the work is too unfinished. That's why good working relationships with reviewers are critical. When relationships are strong, reviewers know the purpose of the review, where the document stands in the development process, and relevant business requirements. Questions about writing skills ought not to arise in that context.

5) *Avoid the crunch time mentality*. It means unnecessary stress for everyone, it can subvert previous good work, and it serves no good purpose. Things come together. The team knows what needs to be done. A well planned document needs to come out on time, but it does not need the crunch time treatment. A reasonable project schedule introduces the document to its public smoothly and happily.

6) *Review the finished document in light of the project's current requirements*. Projects and their supporting documents can evolve a lot during the project's life cycle. Check before publication to make sure project goals and document content are still aligned. No one will say you must rewrite a document late in the game – at least no one should expect that – but you do have a chance to make late improvements if the larger project calls for them.

7) *Be ready to make corrections and updates after publication*. That is the super-advantage of digital publication. With print publications, errors and omissions might stand forever, because you can never withdraw that bound paper document. With digital publication, mistakes disappear, and required updates rapidly appear when you submit the document's next version for publication. Develop a flexible, streamlined publication process that allows for continuous correction.

Apply these general principles or practices to your own requirements and procedures. Company environments, departmental procedures, evolving tools, customer expectations, engineering and marketing requirements: these factors all affect the way writers develop their documents. Nevertheless, basic principles related to preparation of accurate content hold across all these variables. You can improve document quality, and speed of production, if you integrate these general principles into your document development processes.

Nothing Can Eclipse a Good Writer

A couple of recessions ago, U. S. companies started to cut back on the their technical writing departments. Instead of large, stable writing groups, companies hired more contractors as needed, while a small core group tried to hold things together. Then outsourcing became the fashion, where documentation could be had for cheap. When you send development of your technical publications overseas, you bump your ability to communicate with customers a couple of steps down the corporate priority ladder. It confirms the general idea that before you ship your product, you must check off the tech doc box.

So fifteen years ago, during the doldrums that followed the Y2K excitement, you started to hear technical writers say that the profession would not last much longer. It seemed to have no staying power, because no one wanted to hire a technical writer. I argued that companies always need people who can write, which means they need people who can do research and communicate what they learn. These skills are valuable no matter what job label you apply, because if a company can't communicate with its customers, it ceases to exist. Good writers seldom feel unneeded.

Here's an interesting thought, related to the function that writers perform in a company. As more companies evolve toward a service model, where customers subscribe to software services they cannot or do not want to maintain in house, good technical writing becomes altogether more critical. Both customers and internal customer service people need excellent, up to date information, ready to hand, to make the service model work. Because the technology you deliver changes so fast, good communication becomes a key bridge to success in a service model.

On the older model – where you simply sold a product – you could slide with inferior information because your competition's was just as bad, and customers put up with it. When customers pay out a substantial subscription fee every month or quarter, they'll be far less tolerant of an operation that looks even partially incompetent. Moreover, a company cannot give good service if its representatives – who have to learn somehow – do not understand how to make a complicated operation work right for a particular customer. They need easy to use, up to date, and accurate documentation, too. If field service representatives don't know what they are doing, customers become impatient fast, and may even change vendors.

Ultimately customers don't care how their vendors execute a service model. They just want key IT and software operations to be totally reliable, easy to accomplish, and free of any maintenance cost above the subscription fee. All of that does not happen with inferior documentation, nor does it happen without competent, technically proficient communicators. Writers, who seemed headed for oblivion a decade and a half ago, have reemerged as content developers and strategists in a business environment that needs superior technical communication skills. So writers have become important people!

Why You Should Write Professionally

My intention is to write about practical issues that arise for writers, editors, and content managers, in particular people who work with technical content. Some practical issues raise narrow questions of procedure; others raise larger questions about why good craftsmanship and clear communication are worthwhile to begin with. As you think about what *you* would like to write about, give yourself some room. You may find you write about subjects you did not even know interested you that much, until you started to write about them.

I've been a consultant for a long time. Consultants get to work with engineers from many different fields. Generally engineers, like the rest of us, have a lot to say. They have skills other people need, but their expertise may be hard to understand, and therefore hard to remember. The need to convey engineering ideas and designs professionally, in written form, acquires extra importance – otherwise potential customers won't readily grasp what you can do for them. Prospects often go to a recruiter with a job description: "Please find someone who can do that." Better if the customer in need calls the consulting engineer, based on the engineer's reputation in the field.

Standard advice for independent experts is to establish your reputation both through your work, and via what you write. Offer free advice and practical guidance, show that you have expertise in your field, and that you can communicate it to others. Then people remember you when they need an expert with your skills.

Though engineers know writing articles, books, and commentary can help them establish a reputation, and more specifically communicate what they know to prospective clients, they have good reasons not to publish their work. One reason, of course, is shortage of time. When difficult projects occupy your days, you won't likely write technical articles at night. Where to publish your work presents a second obstacle. A third question concerns quality and clarity, since some engineers seem to have convinced themselves they can't write well.

I do not think the last reason is true. Engineers as a group can write as well as members of any other group. Take another profession for comparison: some attorneys prepare better legal documents than others. In a field like that, poor writing skills will handicap your advancement, perhaps more so than in engineering. Yet anyone – no matter one's proficiency – can become a better writer. As with any skill, you learn how to communicate clearly with practice. To suggest that engineers as a group can't write looks suspiciously like the sort of professional fiction that relieves you from trying to improve.

The first two reasons – where to find the time and where to publish your work – require a little more attention. They are not excuses so much as practical problems.

I used to fret too that my non-paid professional activities slipped to nearly zero during periods of active involvement with a project. Now I recognize that consultants have to operate that way. Even if you do stay active during a project, the likelihood of lining up a new project as you finish the current one is not so high. So you know you can set aside time between projects for those non-paid activities that didn't fit as you worked long days. Writing articles about professional topics that interest you belong in that category. In fact, don't think of professional writing as non-paid: it supports your practice, and helps you secure your next project.

Publication posed some difficult problems before the digital era. Unless you knew an editor or published regularly somewhere, publication efforts could be extensive, thankless and even exhausting, with uncertain results. Today the publication process remains somewhat troublesome, but for different reasons.

Professionals used to publish their work in trade journals. Those publications, like every other paper periodical, are scarce these days. If you want people to read your work, you need to put it online, even though millions of other people do the same thing.

You don't have the imprimatur of an established, edited journal to recommend your thoughts to readers any longer. You have to promote your own work, modest though the work and the promotional efforts may be. If your thoughts have intrinsic worth, however, what you publish will serve your purposes: to help others, and to build your own reputation as you do so.

If you have already published your work online, you have a sense of the channels you prefer, to reach the people you want to reach. If you have not published your thoughts online, and believe your career prospects would improve if you did, learn how to do blog posts. Blog posts are nothing more than short articles, published in a particular way. I like to write about politics and current affairs on the side, so I maintain a blog for that purpose. I also write a lot about writing, as you an see from this book. Publishing articles online gives me a feel for the satisfactions and difficulties of the blogger's medium. A key plus is ease of use. A key drawback is that blog promotion is no easier than promotion of anything else in a teeming digital environment. You can publish for a long time with few readers.

A few years ago LinkedIn decided to make a publishing platform available to everyone on the site. That was significant. Due to LinkedIn's original purpose as a business networking site, the audience you want to reach when you publish advice or other professional content exists right where you publish your article. Moreover, LinkedIn made its publishing tools about as simple as it could. As a text editor, the platform has all that it needs. The end product looks like a well formed article, with sharing and commenting tools you expect.

One more thing to note about short articles: you can reuse them easily. Wherever they first appear, you can repost them elsewhere. Most importantly, you can post your articles at your own website. If you don't have a site, consider making one, even if it is only one page. Tools for site setup and development make the process easy now. If you plan to work only for other companies during your career, or develop your personal brand, to pick up the latest marketing idea, you need the latitude of a site you own.

Professional websites or blogs come under consideration here because they serve as a place where you can publish your articles over time. When you correspond with colleagues, you can send an easy to remember links to your own site, rather than old, possibly broken and hard to find links to other sites. Once people arrive at your site, they can easily visit other pages to become acquainted with your work. Most importantly, your publications are under your direct control when you publish them at a site that you own. Your only constraints are the site's publishing tools. Aside from creative control at publication time, you can update your articles as you keep up with your field: make corrections and revisions, incorporate feedback, add developments, links, and images to keep the content fresh. For myself, I like to work on new stuff, but I'm also happy to know I can revisit older material.

To circle back, people write for several reasons, some of them personal, some of them professional. Relatively new publishing tools, as well as new expectations about how we present our ideas and where we publish them, put professional communication within everyone's reach now. The internet is the great leveler, and everything about professional publishing is more informal than it used to be. Growth in knowledge and improvement of outcomes accompany advancement in every area, engineering or otherwise. All of this progress requires good leadership. You can direct other people's attention to things you believe are important, and perhaps most pertinently, help them achieve professional growth of their own. If you contribute to your field via simple, short articles, you'll be happy to hear your colleagues say, "I've seen your posts."

Demystification of the Writing Process

A writer-in-residence at a college where I taught said that writing instructors can demystify the writing process. Until that point, I had not really thought of writing as a mysterious process, just a difficult one. Now an expert suggested that it was not only difficult, but also inaccessible if one did not have a guide to its mysteries.

That struck me as true at the time, but I'm not sure why it would be true. Writing only appears mysterious because people who teach it sometimes make it harder than it actually is. Compare writing to the building trades. I admire people who know how to build things. The whole process of building a house, or an addition, or doing a complete remodel used to seem almost like magic to me. I certainly didn't know how to do it. Then I witnessed the process in my own house, and could see that these were skills one could learn. That didn't mean I would learn them, but the building process didn't seem so mysterious anymore. I had watched someone do it.

Writing is similar in some ways. Like building, it is a craft. It requires skill, or know-how that does not come in a day. The mystifying part about writing is the part you can't see. You have to think about what you want to write, and the contents of your mind are invisible. That invisibility is not so different from the building process. A good craftsman works from a coherent set of plans – plans that originate in one's imagination before they become drawings. After you plan a building project, you hold a vision of the finished project in your mind as you undertake construction. In all of these respects, writing and construction parallel one another.

Some say writing is thinking. No wonder, then, that the invisible work of literary creation appears mysterious! After all, writing is the craft of transforming ephemeral thoughts into something more permanent – something that lasts longer than the swift movements of an active mind. You can imagine a new room for your house, or a number of rooms, but until you build them they don't exist for anyone but yourself. The same goes for writing. Your thoughts exist only for you until you write them down.

Speech may help others participate in your thoughts, but it does not resolve the essential impermanence of thought. Talking to other people is in fact a powerful form of communication and persuasion. Nevertheless, verbal utterances are far more transitory than anything you have written. Think of a tune you might hear from the throat of a bird. It is beautiful, but has no effect on anyone except listeners who happen to be present. The craft of writing gives people the power to make their thoughts durable, and accessible to anyone.

One more observation is necessary before we consider the process of writing in a business and engineering environment. Writing instructors, coaches, editors, publishers – even the mysterious and sometimes mystified writers – remind us that no specific method of writing works for everyone. We all have our own ways of working. Nevertheless, we still distinguish between well written and poorly written pieces, and we can perceive these differences when we read a document. Can't we trace these differences in quality to the writer's methods? Good craftsmanship depends on the proper application of your know-how to create a written product. If that is the case, why would writers who practice their craft with devotion say you go by the rules? Do practices among good writers *differ* that much?

Here a comparison with cooking is helpful. When you first learn to cook, you do follow recipes. You have to follow the rules pretty carefully if you want to create something you can serve to other people. Try to be too creative – that is, depart from the recipe – when you are a beginner, and you will not achieve good results. With experience, though, you develop your own methods – ways of doing things that work for you. You begin to learn when you can vary a recipe, try a different technique, plan a little more loosely, and eventually create your own recipes.

Writing works that way, too. To take a simple example: after you have some experience, you need not outline your piece every time you sit down to write. If you have thought about the subject sufficiently, you can write something reasonably well structured without outlining your thoughts first. Sometimes your piece follows a structure that someone else has developed, or that you developed some time ago. Nevertheless, if you skip writing an outline, or some planning document that serves the same function, you may encounter difficulties with your writing project. Experience makes you aware of those difficulties. It also makes you more tolerant of them, and helps you work around them.

What do these remarks about experience tell us about the nature of writing as a human activity. First and most obvious, writing activities employ thoughts as their primary input. Writing processes thoughts to turn mental phenomena into verbal structures. In that light, how to produce any kind of document need not be a mystery. As with other crafts, magical qualities dissipate as you learn or become familiar with the skills required. Second, different kinds of writing require different kinds of skills. Business writing differs from fictional storytelling, which differs from poetry, which differs from legal writing. Skills required to build a boat differ from skills required to construct an addition to your house, though both projects require some skill in carpentry. Third, the *only* method anyone has ever used to learn and acquire a skill is practice. Musicians know that. Athletes know it. Craftsmen in all the building and artisanal trades know it. Writers know it, too. You cannot learn to write, unless you write. When you do, each skill you learn, and each improvement you make, prove that mysteries eventually yield to competence.

Here's a concluding thought to add some motivation. To advance your career, you need to know how to write. If you cannot write, you will reach a point where you cannot advance further. If you develop your ability to write well, you can overcome a lot of obstacles. Everyone appreciates the centrality of writing; few appreciate the elements of craftsmanship that make writing effective in the first place. If you grasp and then master these elements of craftsmanship, you hold the keys for making your thoughts durable, persuasive, and of practical use for anyone who cares to read them.

Radical Necessity of Version Control

Version control falls under the heading of *Housekeeping: How to Keep Your Publications Shop Tidy*. Some years ago we saw plenty of books about decluttering: your closets, your basement, your kitchen, your bedrooms, your garage, your recreation room or family room, your attic. The idea took hold that detritus from every stage of life swamped us: if you don't free yourself now, you'll go under and never appear in public again. To increase the sense of urgency, declutterers suggested that if your house ain't tidy, what can you say about the rest of your life? Get your house in order, and everything else will improve.

Well I won't argue with that here. Let's see how these ideas apply to writing. For business documents and document repositories, version control imposes and maintains order. Nancy Allison gave a talk recently called *Disaster Recovery: Fixing a Documentation Mess*. She begins: "Do you ever feel like you've just been handed a giant mess? The documentation is in complete disarray and needs to be tidied up... [I have] a particular fondness for wading into a documentation catastrophe and restoring order." If you have worked in the field of technical publications for even a short time, you know what she's talking about.

Near the end of this book, I mention five housekeeping practices that help you keep things squared away and under control. That's the army ideal: beds made in the morning, dishes clean after every meal, uniform crisp, shoes polished, floors mopped and lockers in order. Engineers and other technical people may not care for the army life, but if disorderliness and a sprawling sense of chaos at the door cause you anxiety or just uneasiness, you start to think about how to shape things up. Knowing how to handle multiple versions of the same document over long time spans gives you mastery over these problems.

To get started, ask what should I consider if I'm about to select a version control system for my shop? That's a hypothetical question, because most shops have to live with the system they already have in place. For good reasons, most operations pause before they change to a new version control system. At the same time, changing to a new system may not be as hard as you think. Tools have improved over ten years and more. Besides, the hypothetical question is only a point of departure. I don't want to advocate that you change your version control system. The one you have may serve your needs well. "What should I consider?" questions help us think about what we might want from any version control system we may try – and what we want to avoid.

By now we're ready to say in general what a version control system does. At its simplest, it tracks a document through its life cycle. It is not, however, merely a software tool. A content management system, of which versioning is a part, comprehends more than the software used to implement it.

One of the worst experiences for any writer is to find suddenly that you don't know which version of a document is your latest. Or you encounter another member of this unpleasant family: you can't find the latest version; your versions have branched, so you have two or more latest versions; team members tried to reconcile two versions, and you can't tell where they left off; you resume work on a version and can't tell what changes other people have made; you overwrite changes in the latest version by accident, or someone accidentally overwrites your latest changes. Everyone has dealt with at least one of these situations. Everyone hopes to avoid them, because they feel like a waste of time. No one wants to solve problems that could have been avoided.

A long time ago, project managers and software specialists designed version control systems to prevent these time-consuming, demoralizing detours. Software development teams are often large: without a version control system, team members cannot collaborate. The same goes for teams that produce technical publications. Because requirements for software builds and technical publications seemed to parallel each other, technical writers often dropped their files into the same folder structure the developers used. That meant they used the same version control system, too.

I don't need to explain all the reasons that arrangement did not work so well. It took a little time, but people began to recognize that everyone – developers, writers, quality assurance, managers, and engineering support – would do better if the pubs team managed their files separately from the software files. Gradually software repositories and document libraries began to develop their own version control requirements.

Let's consider five elements of a full-featured document versioning system: 1) automatic file backup, 2) file locking or something equivalent, 3) convenient file sharing and distribution, 4) revision history, and 5) effective integration with authoring and publication tools. If a document versioning system does not incorporate these capabilities, it probably won't meet the needs of a team larger than two.

Typically document versioning comes built into content management systems, which can run into some money. Some version control systems are standalone, and they cost less. Some are free, and some are free with a paid version for more features. Partly because no standard option exists, a fair number of shops do not use a version control system you can name. Others use old but adaptable systems that, come what may, have served reasonably well for as long as anyone can remember. Some shops tolerate legacy systems that may not agree with requirements and workflows of cloud computing. As a planner, take all of your company's and your shop's needs into account as you investigate how various version control systems contribute to efficient document management. Business analysts look for a problem's root cause. Effective version control counts as a radical necessity, because without it, you continually feel on the edge of disaster recovery mode.

Why Should I Use Context Sensitive Help?

Context sensitive help has matured as content-rich, online help systems have matured. It even has its own acronym now: CSH. When something has its own acronym, you know it has arrived. It has proven its worth to help people learn complex software in diverse environments. Applications, whether web-based or locally hosted, have different types of context sensitive help available. Moreover, developers and help authors can readily integrate it with cloud-based applications.

Not so long ago, online help often installed with the software as a compiled CHM file that came with its own browser and resided on your local drive. Context sensitive help was somewhat more impractical for authors in that environment. You could incorporate it in your application, but it felt just cumbersome enough that you generally wanted to avoid it, or keep it to a minimum. Now most HTML help files live on servers, so you can be more creative about supplying context sensitive help, even aggressive if you like. You needn't hang back, because integration of the required HTML help files with the software does not feel hard.

Most people know what context sensitive help is because they use it all the time. They rely on it, even if they don't see it from the back end. Yet for help authors the concept can get away from you, because it refers to more than one thing. For users, the idea is simple: you click a help icon or some other symbol to open help that pertains to your location in the interface. The location, or context, could be the entire screen, a panel or dialog box, a particular field or button, or any portion of the interface that might require explanation. The big advantage of context sensitive help is that you don't need to navigate your way to information you need. On the other side, context sensitive help is not designed to explain an entire workflow, which usually requires interaction with a number of locations in the interface. The same goes for concepts and background information users need to understand what they are doing. You do not look for this kind of information in context sensitive help.

For engineers and help authors – that is, for developers who work on the application's back end – context sensitive help may still seem a little difficult to deploy. That's especially true now that companies and service providers deploy applications in so many different environments. Consequently, engineers must test online help along with the rest of the software. So we want to define context sensitive help in a way that makes sense to engineers and product managers, and discuss briefly the options help developers have when they think about how to implement context sensitive help for their applications.

Context sensitive help works because the application contains a link between the user's location in the interface, and help relevant to that location. Specifically, when a user clicks to request help, the application knows which HTML help file to serve. It knows because developers create a link between the user's context and the file. Because these files, and user requests that open them, are not part of the application's main work flow, developers generally integrate the files as they test the application and prepare it for deployment. When they integrate context sensitive help, they incorporate references to the help files in the code. These links tell the software which help file to open, for each item users might click to request help.

The button might be a help button in the upper right portion of the page. In that case, CSH would open a help topic to give an overview of the page, or to orient users who may not be well oriented when they arrive. Alternately, an icon may be a question mark or information symbol, located at a place on the screen where users probably need guidance. Lastly, we have all learned to rely on tooltips that appear when you hover over a menu selection, a data field, or any other clickable item on a screen.

Short as they are, these ubiquitous tips make up the most familiar form of context sensitive help.

If you need more space than a tooltip normally offers, you have a presentation choice to make. Do you want to present your material in a pop-up box, or take users straight to a topic in the online help? A pop-up is not a bad option: you can present basic guidance there, then include one or more links to more comprehensive help topics. If you take users directly to an online help topic for any context sensitive help request, make sure the content you show clearly relates to the clicked item. Users lose patience fast if they need information about a narrow point, and you ask them to scan through a lot of material not relevant to their question.

Developers conscious of good software design rightly seek a natural flow between what users see on the screen and the talk they want to accomplish. When you open an application, you typically want to accomplish something specific. You are eager to learn the correct procedure, if you do not already know it. The learning process is enjoyable when it proceeds efficiently. Developers do not want people to get stuck, so they try to guide users through the steps required to complete a task. When we say that software is intuitive, we mean that flow from one step to the next in a procedure feels effortless. You know what comes next. Sometimes a procedure is quite complex, or a new user needs reassurance. Sometimes an experienced user needs to learn a part of the application not used before. In all of these cases, context sensitive help may offer all the guidance people need, or initiate a productive learning process.

In the end, developers and help authors who incorporate context sensitive help integrate online learning resources with their applications. Opening a pop-up in response to a specific click is not technically difficult, but it does require a little more care, planning, and maintenance than deploying a help topic that stands by itself. Standalone help has its place, too, but users are accustomed now to fast learning. For that, they require help resources that fit the just-in-time model: software supplies just the right information, at just the right location, exactly when the user needs it. Context sensitive help, in all its forms, lets software developers and help authors do that.

RTFM: Acronym Whose Time Never Came

Today I actually saw the acronym RTFM in a post about learning how to use a software application. You remember that one: Read the F**king Manual. I should say that the author of the post used the acronym lightly, not as a put-down. Nevertheless, if you produce a manual for your software or hardware with expectations customers will read it, you are seriously mistaken about a lot of things related to technical learning. I used to write manuals for a living. I don't write them anymore, because for the most part, people do not read them.

I should define what I mean by a manual. It takes the form of a book, often fifty pages or more. These days it is usually a PDF, though other digital formats are possible. It has a cover or title page. It has front matter and back matter. The table of contents reveals the book's organization. Organization of chapters and sections is linear and rational, as you might expect in a textbook. You generally consult the material in order. A manual is not organized like a cookbook, where you find the recipe you need and ignore the rest. In these ways, books differ from the various online learning systems that people have developed over the last decade or so – online learning systems where you find the information you need at the moment, and use it to solve your current problem.

Food Processor, and a Bag of CDs

Let me tell you a story from the holidays, when we visited family in DC. My wife and son were in the kitchen, preparing dinner. My son, as savvy about equipment and technical requirements as they come, and a good cook to boot, pulled out a new food processor that had seen little or no use. Food processors have interlocks to prevent them from operating until every part is perfectly aligned. If you sell an appliance with a whirling blade inside, you want to keep customers safe – then they don't sue you. The blade does not turn until you fit the bowl, cover and base together in some secret way that only the designers know. I say secret because for this model, designers of the appliance placed no markings on the parts to show how they fit together.

Everyone who uses a food processor knows about interlocks. You have to pay close attention to each part to find the magic fit. Yet the designers apparently wanted to make a puzzle out of the whole thing. They build their appliance so as to make a mystery, or a puzzle. They may have thought, "Well it's all explained in the manual," but that reasoning is mistaken. You do not need a manual to assemble the pieces of a properly designed food processor. People do not save manuals for all the appliances that arrive in their house. When you have some vegetables you want to slice, you don't want to go search for a booklet that you're not even sure exists anymore.

Eventually my son Googled the answer to the problem from his phone. It took a bit of research, but he found the information he needed. I expect he thought, "I should have done this earlier." Instructions in one form or another need to be on the internet if you want customers to find them. They need to show up in a simple search that uses the product name. If the manufacturer did not take trouble to supply instructions, someone else out there probably has an answer for you. People expect to find their answer faster with their phone or computer. If the manufacturer did publish a manual, or an instruction sheet, and the owner manages to find it, you still have to navigate through the manual to find what you need. Typically, you scan past multiple safety warnings, included to comply with legal requirements, or to fend off personal injury claims. By contrast, you want a clean, one- or two-click path from question to answer, or from problem to solution. If you want your customers to use your learning materials, they have to be superior to – and accessible as – the internet.

I think about these things because I worked for a company not so long ago that produces manuals for its laboratory instruments. It ships these manuals as PDF files on compact disks. It observes punctilious but ultimately pointless procedures to prepare these doc CDs, in order to deliver documents right in the box, with the instrument. Since the equipment requires special knowledge to set up and operate, they sincerely hope customers place the doc CD in a computer, find and open the correct PDF file, then turn to page one before they do anything with the equipment. Customers will be happy because their expensive new instrument arrives with thorough instructions.

How do customers actually behave when they unpack their equipment? They typically throw the plastic bag full of CDs – disks full of drivers, lab applications, and documents – up onto a shelf! They don't even open the bag, let alone find the doc CD. Instructions in a manual that comes in the box may comply with government regulations – regs written decades ago – but it does not comport with the way people learn now. When was the last time you bought something new, and learned how to use it by reading instructions from a manual stored on a CD? We have better teaching and learning methods now.

More disheartening, people at this conscientious company did not grasp the fate of their carefully prepared documentation, until they observed customers unpack a new piece of equipment. You can't criticize the effort required for first-hand observation, but the company was stuck in a doc time warp from a generation ago, when CDs were bright and shiny and gee-whiz. Even after they saw what happened to that bag of CDs out of the box, they continued to deliver their documents the same way! You remember when companies used to send CDs in the mail. We threw them out, and that was when CDs were still novel. Send your customers a CD now and they'll think, "What, they want me to load this? All I have here is my phone!" You may as well send a five-and-a-quarter inch floppy disk for a drive they've never seen.

Do not depend on CDs, paper manuals, or anything not easily findable with a mobile device, for your daily bread. Your hard work will wind up on the top shelf, unopened and unread. Find a way to teach customers how to use your products some other way, because they will not RTFM. The people who invented that acronym thought they were cool and a bit superior – techies who already knew it all. Maybe they *did* know a lot, but it's not cool to use a profane put-down to remind others that you know more than they do. Neither is it cool to hand your new customers a fat PDF with tons of information in it with curt advice: "Here, come back after you've read this." You have plenty of competitors who understand how to manage technical learning better than that.

Information Design and User Experience

Online response to my initial thoughts about manuals was swift and sure. One thing you can say about digital communications: it is fast and people let you know what they think. More than one commenter said that manuals still have a place – some customers still like to see them as part of a company's communications arsenal. Others generally agreed that manuals don't readily fit the learning methods that have developed in an age of broadband, mobile communications. Here are some remarks from Ellen Ashdown in the latter category:

"I think I own that food processor. The food processor tale is also a story about lousy product design, which can't always be fixed by good documentation. In my experience, a typical user interaction with documentation looks like this: 1) customer experiences a problem; 2) customer attempts to figure it out; 3) customer gets frustrated; 4) customer figures it out, quits in disgust, goes to the documentation, calls or emails support, or goes to another source, such as Google.

"If they go to the documentation, most people have a specific topic or question, and need to be able to locate that and only that information quickly, or they choose another option. If you're constantly telling your users to RTFM, look for gaps in your documentation and training, and in how you're presenting your data.

"Information design and the user experience for documentation is still a huge gap for a lot of companies. If you understand how and why customers go to the documentation, you can make it easy for them to get their answers in the shortest time possible, which is what they want. It may be quite different for each customer, which is why single sourcing is such a great tool. You're always going to have customers who want to get the answer from a real person, and whose first reaction is to pick up a phone to call your support team. That's never going to change.

"In light of that, here's a worthy practice. Distribute your documentation to your field support team in an organized way. Then, when customers call in with a question you know the answer to, your team has exactly the information they need to give them the answer right away. It adds value to your documentation when you use the same content your team generates for clients, to provide information to your customer support team. In this case, the content serves as a knowledge base or support reference system for field application engineers, and every other person who helps customers succeed with your company's products."

Two War Stories

Now let me tell a couple of war stories. War stories are great, because they tell how you fought the good fight, and you're the hero of the tale. Your listeners may not believe you, but then, they weren't there.

I tell these stories with an emphasis on process. In both cases, I was the tech pubs manager, and a one-person shop, so I had an interest in those issues. In the first instance I tried to change the company's practices, but too many other factors interfered to make the effort successful. In the second instance, I just had to be patient to see things work out.

Let's start with company X, in the semi-conductor industry. The company designs chips that serve as the controller – the central processing unit – for multi-function printers. It tests those chips on a variety of reference boards, but in the end, engineers who design printers need to make those controllers work in their own companies' products. That means company X supplies essential information about the chip to their customers' engineers, so they can design and build high-quality printers around the chip.

Well, the company supplied essential information and then some. The one-inch square silicon wafer shipped with a heavy register specification: nearly eight hundred pages of small print. It came with a software development kit. The kit had a manual over twelve-hundred pages long. That was about two thousand pages total, which created a huge *Where's Waldo* problem for customers. The nugget of information they needed at a particular point in the design process hid under a mountain of distracting data that had no relevance to the engineer's question of the moment. The engineer would call for help, often from the other side of the world. Sometimes the implicit response to his query was, "Have you read the register specification?"

You do *not* want to ask a question like that of your customers! They are stuck. They do not want to sift through amazing amounts of data you threw at them because you did not want to trouble yourself to decide what customers had to know, out of all the material that proved useful at some point during your own design process. Customers do not need to know everything you know.

I'll admit that boiling down the register specification would have been a time-consuming process. A company could easily say that it was not worth the benefit, especially since it wanted to have that information on record for its own engineers. What customers really needed, beyond the chip's pinout diagram, was accurate, crisp documentation of the API supplied in the software development kit. That information could have been distributed right with the API's files, and produced online using an open-source tool like doxygen. Then design engineers could easily find information they need to make other circuitry and components communicate with the printer's controller. You want to integrate basic information about how to use the API's functions with the software development kit, not present it in a long PDF that busy engineers may be reluctant to open.

The company did not care to do it. Not so surprisingly, company X's aim to make its controllers part of millions of printers and other image processing devices worldwide did not work out.

The second story is easier to tell, as it's a success story for document integration. Company Y sold a set of tools to transform platform-independent models into embedded software. You could use the toolset to develop detailed specifications for the software, package by package, then transform the model into code for a specific platform. For instance, you could develop a signal processing model for a radar system – a system that performs the same basic functions no matter what antenna you use – then generate code that accurately processes signals for a specific platform.

The company decided to use a software development environment called Eclipse to prepare its toolset for commercial distribution. That was a good choice: anyone can download Eclipse from the internet. Moreover, IBM supports it. Most important, Eclipse helps to streamline the toolset's distribution. Among its capabilities – a great benefit for me, the online help developer – were effective documentation tools. You could readily create a table of contents using XML, and you could prepare help topics in the same environment as the toolset. You did not even have to look far for a template, as Eclipse's own help system served well as model for other online help you might want to develop.

Company Y's experience illustrates what to seek as you design what we now call customer experience. You want your customers to have information they need a couple of clicks away. Don't make them look around for CDs or navigate long PDFs. Above all, avoid *Where's Waldo* searches once you guide them to the correct location. People like Google because it filters information they need from everything else on the internet. You want to supply better information, and faster, than your customer can obtain with a Google search. If you do, your documentation will be so concise and interactive, and so accessible, that it helps customers refine their questions as they search for answers.

That's enough for stories. It is actually not that hard to answer people's questions. Harder is to organize information for complicated, sophisticated products that operate via invisible software commands, signal pathways, and data flows. Effective, timely, targeted delivery of information is also not easy. Well-intentioned companies want to develop processes that communicate information in flux, to customers whose own needs change rapidly, but they have found that ideal a challenge. Yet we have tools to accomplish these things, and we have not lost our appreciation of simplicity whilst we harry ourselves with complicated problems. We're still mindful of how to make things work, elegantly and seamlessly. Bring out your iPhone or Galaxy to be reminded of that.

Concluding Thoughts: Good Housekeeping

We've talked about document formats and delivery methods, and the processes required both to develop and to distribute different types of publications for customers. To start, we suggested that you should not expect your customers to read traditional manuals in order to use your products. Then we discussed alternate processes and formats to communicate technical information to customers. That's the goal after all: communicate essential information to people who want to benefit from what you sell.

Let's finish with a look at several administrative or housekeeping matters to consider as you manage digital content. These principals apply to management of all kinds of material, from traditional manuals all the way to internet-friendly, distributed information. We like our mental spaces as well as our work areas to be clean and tidy, with items we need easily retrievable, and basic processes on automatic. These goals all apply to our interactions with digital content, especially when we create the content. Here are five practices to follow:

- Develop consistent file naming conventions and storage principles.

- Streamline production processes.

- Use a version control system.

- Do not maintain two copies of the same content in two different locations.

- Pay attention to your primary distribution channels.

The table below elaborates a bit on each of these points:

Document Administration	Description
Data retrieval	Develop consistent file naming conventions and storage principles. Then you can scan long lists of files and folders, or enter search terms, with confidence you will locate exactly what you need.
Production processes	Streamline production processes. Design them for accuracy and speed. That means simple, easy-to-maintain templates; simple, easy-to-follow procedures; and unobtrusive error-checking for quality assurance.
Version control	Use a version control system that runs in the background, and integrates well with your other tools. It should be especially well adapted for document control.
Single source	Do not maintain two copies of the same content in two different locations. Single-sourcing across an entire enterprise is still a holy grail, but you can practice it in your own domain. If you need to make an update, make it once, in one source document.
Distribution channels	Pay attention to your primary distribution channels. If your audiences – external and internal – tell you they do not have required information, when and where they expect it, look for shortcomings in your production and distribution plan.

These five practices sound self-evident when you write them down, but in fact they are a challenge for companies of all sizes, especially for large ones. Why *do* practices that seek simplicity, accuracy and speed seem to become complex so readily? Well, people come and go, products and marketing strategies change, some tools work well and others do not, leadership and working groups change, customer requirements push companies in multiple directions, internal conflicts and tensions develop. If problems come piecemeal, so do the solutions.

Within shifting environments, complexity even looks attractive at times, but mostly companies try to maintain simple, consistent practices. The simplest and most consistent way to accomplish tasks may appear to be the way you accomplished them in the past. Merely doing what you've always done, however, may fail you, because what you've always done doesn't match your current goals, market, or operating environment. Tried and true methods become rigid, not rigorous, while plans that used to embrace change now stave it off.

Competitive, forward-looking firms account for change in all their business plans. Otherwise you end up hamstrung with procedures and tools and tired practices that used to work, or that someone thought would work, but that only cause problems when you try to meet challenges coming into view. Among those challenges, communication strategies and practices occupy a central position. If they don't work, little else does.

About the Author

Steven Greffenius graduated from Reed College with a degree in history, and later from the University of Iowa with a Ph.D. in political science. In between he served as electronics material officer aboard USS KIRK (FF-1087) in the Western Pacific.

Currently, Steve lives with his family in Westwood, Massachusetts, outside of Boston. He founded Puzzle Mountain Digital, PuzzleMTN.com, to publish technical as well as non-technical work. *RTFM: Practical Advice for Smart Writers* is his eleventh book as author or editor.

www.ingramcontent.com/pod-product-compliance
Lightning Source LLC
Chambersburg PA
CBHW032018190326
41520CB00007B/530